— for the people
of Portsmouth,
New Hampshire

Best Always

Sandy Chilcote   20 November 1996

Earththings

Sandy Chilcote

Acknowledgements: To TickleAce magazine
for publishing some of these poems --
to the Parks and Natural Areas Division
and Mr. A. Glen Ryan for the illustrations
of Labrador tea

Published by: The Ashuanipi Press, Ltd.
6 Lomond Street, Corner Brook A2H 3A9

Printed by: Commercial Printing
Corner Brook, Newfoundland, Canada

in cooperation with **R3** Books
P.O. Box 8600
St. John's, Newfoundland, Canada
A1B 3T7

Earththings
first printing, 1996

ISBN No. 0-920884-49-0

for my family and friends

and for Labrador and Newfoundland,
    their people and places,
    the country, and for all
    the other much-loved people
    and places

Earththings
leafthings small
once and only things

Appreciation
Is the single greatest act
The best we can do
The most that can be expected
Looking at a pebble
And seeing its words

Sounds to images
Words to images to sounds
To words --

The meaning of things is
Things

Even my words surrender

How does one define being blest?

I know -- Kathryn Kuhlman, the faith healer, defines it
one way

Perhaps there is another of being so proud of being
human that even the humility of believing in God
is not attractive

Can anyone love the courage of mortality so much?

Where are the sources
The fountains
The beginnings of great rivers?
Among reeds
Mountain lakes
Winds --
It is the silent tilt of the land
That begins a river

They make their nests
Where there are few sharp edges
Where the rains can be covered
By their feathers
And the wind is not too strog
They build
In the face of human jealousy
And destruction

The worst rain is
The rain in the soul
Cold and icy,
Freezing the heart
With unkindness --
Hands turned down
Blankly

Weeping ice in her long tresses
A comet goes, visiting stars
And suns and eyes that gaze
Creating memories
And she bright again now in
Some distant, deep shadow

Inquiry cannot do enough for love
Enough for oranges, apples,
Limes
Inquiry would do enough for us all
But if it cannot do
Enough for seaweed, shores
And catching crabs in baskets on the beach
It cannot do nearly
Enough for lobstermen either --
Fish of the sea kept wishing
And asking what it
Could do for them
And it was only as much as
It could do for birds
Or even feathers --
The pinions for pens
Were not enough --
Inquiry just could not do --
Yet pens sometimes try
As dolphins, to lead
When there is only a chance
In a word

Tracks of mice
Laced in the snow
They search
From one brown
Bareness
To another
And a rabbit
Jumped through
The foot of snow
To the shade
Of pines
In this meadow
Is no grass
In one place
A squirrel dug in
To grass
And tunnelled out
But the scurrying
Mice
Weave wildly
In the vast places

Owls can be ceramic or china
Or owls can have eyes as big as knuckles
And sit in the hemlocks
Winking
While the wind blows

The thousand lovely faces
Of mimic moon passing
Quickly as one
In the golden ring behind the cloud sheet
The white screen of blue night

Hydrangia's five hundred mittens
Tell me
Given to me, readying me for winter

Dusk
The cutting edge of night
Young frogs singing
Like sharpening knives

A sheet of ice on the cold
Black autumn water
Surrounded by the dry skeletons
Of trees after the flooding
Of a beaver dam
And hung with the fanciful grey
Green apparel of lichens
And branching mosses
Even the color of pink spores
All with the quietness of
A past age

As I think on marsh thickets
Bumpy with snow
My thoughts eat grass
Like the caribou migrating

The horse
Ridden simply as the Bedouin
Rides
Without stirrups or bit
To insult him
The horse strong
Like the mystery of life

Dry flowers
Grow out of
Snow
Snow is piled
On bent limbs
Why do they cut down
My forest
While the snow
Is gentle

Me in a black coat
A raven singing out
Quietness
Black pines
Above
The black roofs
Of city houses
I walk
Through a foot of snow
In the country
A mile
Before I come
To tracks from the sawmill
I turn away
Before I meet them

When I cry
May I cry like the cedars
With grace and beauty
Living like them

Let my petals fall
Soft love
I will not burn

An old cradle
Rocks out youth
Rocks flowers
From its soil

It is most wise
To be calm
When the black elves
Scream
In the pines

Little leaf children dancing
Little leaf children
Dancing to nature's force

Can a man's shell
Leave as much beauty on the snow
As a dried flower

A blueberry-eating moose
Was a gift
Standing, frowning and
Curious --
                    did she know
She had wandered towards guns?

Another day
Finding her viscera tossed aside
I mourned among the berries

Snowy darkness
Little plots of white
Like the eyes of the forest

A lichen flower
Fretted like a carnation
Child of mist and rain

Leaning on a cedar staff
I can make universes --
Always like what I see --
Blooming with love
Like the creator's penis
But I stand miles in the forest
Only to give wild geese
And stray men trying to love
The luck of a wayfarer
From a heart of blood

Old knuckles like pebbles
grandmother
Part of my heart that walks
With me up the mountain
We can smile together
From the dirt of the trail

He draws down the sun, looking through tears
At his mother's eyes, hoping for warm darkness
Fearing night's dreams

Whisperings in the morning
My daughter waking up
I touch her soft face and soft hair
How far in the night
Did you go, child?
Farther than I
Deeper
And you found
A threat to your brother
And father
A screaming for mommy
It is a black trough
Of black tongues
But it can also be a mother
With warm kisses
Gentle hands

A voice kept asking what I was
Inside
Well, I was like the snow
Shaped in each flake
Circlings
Framed by a window

If ever, after I have fallen away into
The cold sea of things and stand as I was,
This strange gift is gone, yet shared perhaps,
My cup of water flowing on through the cloth,
As soon given away today as yesterday or tomorrow,
Then I may become as persistent as the sun
Wheeling snow hoops in the courtyard
Before the next door standing quiet and loving
Every moment of these bright circles leaping in the wind

While men work with the hives
Little wagoneers
Wagoning
Bees
        dandelions and the sun
Wagoned
And visited for nectar

Hands reach into the boneless mud
Cupped hands hold
Tears, smiles
The earth folding
Clay and pebble folds
Mother and child

In the womb
Silence
One language

In the cherry tree
Before a storm the wind blows the clay bells
Ringing
In the soft rain
Cool and moist swaying
The sun warms them
Your hands can hardly touch them
Motionless
Cold and whirling snow
Ice and hanging icicles
Always the clay bells
Are the clay bells

The fearsome heat of battle
        spinning bodies
And minds

Can they ever become waterlilies
        again

Maybe in years

if death is an end
it is an end like a tree has
ding ding ding ding ding ding
ding ding ding ding ding
rain drops
a fragile maple leaf
unriffles

Dear gentle rectangle
Bread
Thumped and kneaded with the
Nimble angles of fingers
Then given to the oven
Baked
The smell of wheat in the air
The dough under my fingernails

The blesséd
There are some who are
Stem and leaf

Dragons thumping across the sky
Into the sun
Tails high
Hair on the belly
Light in the eye

Smell of the wood stove
Old grandfather
Your white hair
Is like the ash
Your hands
Delicate
With the smell of skin bracer
And softening creams
Do you live towards your end
Reading the grass
And the dew on your feet
As well as teaching forever
Your grandson to fish?

The vision of my movements

In the tops of the trees

The vision

More than pretending

To see myself in a mirror

Spring
The black-dotted pearls
Of toads and frogs
Strings and jellies
In the pond

The creases
Wrinkles
Under the knot of your tie
Like the creases
In your face

                Sculptured room

        Word place

        Sunning place
                        beach dune

        Hollow -- sea water
                        rushes in

        Rushes out

        Pulling sand

"Daddy" --
"Downstairs"
He cried, sobbing
Leading me by the hand
At three-thirty in the morning
We must feed the birds
My carrying him
And his carrying the seed
His sobs
Stop slowly

Patches of brown leaves
Winding across the short grass
The wind picks up four or five
And tosses them
Into the bare spaces
Nature

Bees in freezing November weather
Furiously kill old workers
Pushing them out into
The cold air

Where do they work
When the pears are
Too rotten to be sweet?
There are still a few
Dandelions

Can you use the earth as wisely as the sun
Or the bees making angles from sun to flower?
Love

On the other side of the earth the sun
Is coming
Sunset
China

Under the big hemlock with the beehives
                    my friend
Loves the many songs
The wind interchanges with the boughs
High and low
Soughings and bleatings of November
That is the new song
Because now the bees
Are quiet

Old princess pine bent with the breaking of the wind
Before the apple trees I respond to your sighs
To the wind
Of your sighs
Darker than the skies of March or November

Humans are like blue and yellow flowers
They perish though they are like
The sky and sun

The land folds in many directions
Beyond this
My dry crooked elm bough
Your simple way is not too hard
Companion
The human part is to become like
Their ideas
The strange coolness of thoughts
And their survey
Sometimes
Allows them to accomplish gracefully
Even the last thing

With the horse's canter
The rhythm of years
I have become like a satchel
Containing scrolls
I remain
What remains of me
Scratched into my mind
On my face etched
Like the scars on a freckled pear
I will remember the royal fish
Who reached deep into the
All-embracing oceans
To find a mouthful of mud

Yes, the earth is still called earth
Not steel
Not asphalt

On apple trees
A few leaves clustered
At the tips of branches
On into the winter

I gave up seeing

Myself

Forever

But I did not give up

From birth

The mirror

Rampaging pook
Down the stairs
Bumpling
On her belly
Down the stairs
Pooka pook

I soar
And when I fall
I know it is life
Packed
And snow
Where is the seed in
The feeding station
Giving up to give
Mystery
Gift

Something new loving me

Saves me every day

Cora

Indians farmed
And sang growing loving
Songs to their corn
Lifting warm hands
To
Green leaf hands

Like my face looking towards
The mountains
A crow coming to rest
In the afternoon
Up in the dry limbs of a
Dead oak
Poetry
Muscle
Crow like a woman
Beak to my beak
Try giving to me
Out here in the wind
An oak leaf dry brown
Another oak leaf to you
And not even twigs between us

Adobe woman of
Millions of wrinkles
Her skin falling into folds on her arms
Her hands
Still pushing out pots
Pots
Utility and love
On a flat stone
Life

Watching bees

Write

Male

Female

One could search forever

And never find one's regeneration

Going uphill after seven miles
Walking
Partly running
Was often like
Dawn inside

Fruits and nuts

bananas and walnuts

Pecans

beets and pears

Tomatoes

mingled with work

       Run and jump

with me in the

Sun

In a dream --
At the zoo bears escaped
Two great bears rushing down
The sidewalk
Men shot them with bullets rather
Than try to save them
Anesthetize them
I felt fear

Across

Fields

Like squares of light

Coming up to me from

Arles

Identical to squares in my bones that

I cannot see

And out of that other body

My eyes gleam

That body into my eyes

Her elbow at the same angle

As her chin

Weaving plane against

Triangle mountain

I cannot see my face, my neck, my back
My jugular hollow
I bare my life to you and
Let you touch me with your mouth
But we are together
One can see a thing best
Being a thing

The seeding, the sprouting

An event you never

      see happening

      Loving

      you feel

Never seeing
My seed going into your womb
The heart I sometimes feel strong
Pulses from
Confident
My face -- white, black, red, brown
Is in the mirror
More the silver consciousness inside me
Than the glass

The mysterious gift
of giving and
                giving up

Snow, lime and leaves
You know there is
Activity
When I throw on hot water
Steam
Comes up from the pile

Will my little apricots live
Standing the winter to
Spread white blossoms
Bright fruit

Scraps of moments -- the
Dump is not in me nor
Between me and
Seeing

Death
Only consciousness can give up itself
Life
Give up life easily at the last
Like a rose giving up its scent

Bone-carved English sparrow with one leg
The other one broken off
You are my emissary from the library
To the forest
These words need shade
And coolness

Wet simple snows tuck under supple pines
And wrap up in a tight ball warm summer senses

In lovely slowness the
Earth collecting fossils
One moment's thought stretched over
Millenniums, billenniums
Light years

Across the ages
Across the past
          furniture
Rocks, benches, Hepplewhite
The lily pad

In this little room, things of my wife
Of my mother, my father
Me
Once my bedroom, now a library
A place of rest
But can I be assertive here
Like dark trees?

Mind songs -- fog
Dendrites going back to brachiopods
Dryads
We are all inside trees, all of us
Detritus of oaks
Offspring of the decorated wells
In the towns we were bred in, born in
Call home

Should one be amused at deity
It has no bounds, no home
It cannot feed on mold
But must settle for ambrosia
Which may be like ambergris
Deity has no hiding place in the sod
It cannot laugh even as a skeleton laughs
It is deity
Within me, to be summoned
A rock with a burning eye
Mysterious
To me I am mysterious

Woodruff, partridge berry
Fringed polygala
With small mouths
With small cool mouths above the strata
The cool descending
Air
Deity has its own perfume
Ambrosia without
Waxy ambergris

A child asleep on his stomach

I looked down at a block of granite

Unpolished in the floor of the art museum

While people rushed on

Not nation or nation,

This person or that

Old grandmother
Gentle, quick of mind
Never ashamed of her body
Always happy to put on fancy clothes
Never caring for innuendos
    Always keeping a little distance from
    Fear and bitterness
For happiness' sake

Where can the eagle go beyond its wings
and eyrie?

Memories of my dead friend
Do not go into the ground
They continue to shape
Where they have shaped

Board of food with trestles on the side
Forever food where I am without any
Giving up -- it is giving up that I
Value most

These poems are little answers --
little fireflies from the gods
that promise light tomorrow --
little answers to death and defeat

My part coming, leaping in
Skirting the crust of snow
Delicate like the temple
Of the skull

Where is a lion simile, a suitable
Metaphor?
Not among living things, in
                        avalanches
Earthquakes
Lost, big, powerful cat

Eskimo soapstone owl

By Aaluk

I care about the stone in my hands

Heavy like a young child

Like a chick I once held in my child hands

Squat

The weight as if it had blood and bones

I care about the owl the bird

Does it live confidently and in good numbers?

The arctic owl

And I care about the hands and mind

Of Aaluk

The man who loved this stone

And made this carving

And loves the owl

Benevolent -- the paw
Wide, heavy, tender, cuffing
Spreading nails, splayed apart
Claws displayed
From sheaths then
Drawn in to cuff

Wine, wassail bowl over-flowing
Whelming over after being
Mixed too full
A spill into a waterfall
Fecund

Animals loving without pretense
Touching, not bothering with words

It is struggling, a bearing of fangs
The leap indomitable, lion and ax
The spade, exposing the earth, slicing
Smooth and silver

The spade hand-forced, earth-fastening and
The chisel tasting the stone like a tongue
Humans struggle, shape, fashion
Lions stalk the Serengeti, the day is on
Like fingers the black branchings of trees
Against the African dawn

A child among other animals

A man among men, a woman among women

A child among other animals

Pristine
symbol-people
of oak trees
oak tree
town

Cottage
where is your snow?
Cottage, your exercise
where is your horse?
Cottage your winding soul
Clever, agile
where is the serpent?
If you can be as tolerant as the serpent
whom, enforcably cultivated, you
Have ever envied
Jealous face
Changing to arms and legs, changing
And using your body with a sense
Of existence
Then there might be a
Cottage

In my poncho (orange) I am bright
In the high mountains
And I am part of oak tree town
And spruce tree town
The earth here
The food

The breast of dawn
With hemlocks for its trim

The body -- cool, firm, relaxed
Stretching -- the dawn blue, orange and
                          red-streaked
Distant and near

               cold, white snow flurrying

How little can hands be -- can fingers disappear
Like lions' claws, sheathed ?
Cuffing cubs
My children

My body a part of this town
Its trees and air
Its beauty
Uncompromising
And renouncing

My friend waving to the cows is my son -- he waited
As patiently as the salt in his blood would allow
He longs to embrace them and become closely acquainte
He is a friend to cows, to "high" cows -- I follow hi
Snakes are "high," some worms "wee," cows "high" --
Reaching with four legs across the land is our deligh

Horses deserve ornament
On the great steppes
In Aegean marshes
And before Troy's walls
Felt and leather, even
Fitting very closely on their ears
Like tassels for llamas of the
Aymara or of the Quechua --
I have only this ink on paper

Mountaintops and sprucetops
Touch fingertips where we may
Never travel
Andean people, part of the mountains
Stretching plateau, valley of Cuzco
With me in this
                    Labrador valley

The chullo hat, pointed with ear-lugs
The montera hat, the round sun shape
Peruvian hats
Mountain and sun
And the llama wool mask hat
To keep the whole face warm
Children wearing the masks
To laugh and play with wooden sticks
As with swords

A bible from the Andes
The same as a seed catalogue of
Vegetables

I look at the mountains

From the town

Leaning against the wind

Wondering at the scrambling of my hair

In October and November
We can see the mountains from the valley
No one can disregard them
No one can reach over and touch them
No one can love them
Yet we do
And from farther away

It is even wonderful that there are people here
White-gold prayer flags flying, silver-gold
        prayer wheels spinning --
Lo Mantang of earthen red-splashed walls, am
        I a visitor
And a monk who never comes and is never
        supplicant?

Locked in the spirit of the dawn
Myself in the center of that hemisphere
Taut, inverted mouth,
I love your hope turned upwards
    in the trees

Carry me
Carry me in a spoon
Of honey
Or in a little word

The heights of trees
Like the heights of my fingers
When I cry out in joy and in sadness

Stars in the ice --
Snow has blown over the water
And caught by the chill
Has made sudden needles

Winter apples on December 31st
Hanging crisp into the next year

I sleep, Wind -- now --
Knowing it is March
I scent the algae in the ponds
The songs of frogs come
As they bob their heads above water
           after three months
I understand the effluvia of spring, and
I cannot kill

Under the tree canopy
A flycatcher flashing
After an insect
And back to the same branch
Otherwise -- dusk

I loved a pebble, then
a dead butterfly
placing them off to the side of the road
I, without myself, looked

In the one I was all that was dead
with the other, I flew from myself
and discovered my hands picking up
wings
wings that leapt into
the night sky

Owls, katydids
Bats fly through the shadows
Into deeper darkness

Radios interrupt
Human speech is not right
At singing summer midnight
All is touch

Nighthawk near the tops of trees
Across the dusk
Swift and graceful -- after
I had turned around to see
More beauty by walking back
Uphill
Please turn around, too

Autumn dawn, warm
Like early spring and forsythia
The fallen leaves made redder
            by the sun

The battle. Battling
They live elsewhere
And they summon up
Only themselves --
A silvery thread in emptiness --
Only a few can touch it
            when they wish

Sometimes
    the child smiles
    and tells
    Exactly
What she is loving

Dancing --
What is the body like
That is worthy to be among
The stars
Motioning as luminously
As confidently eternal
As truly finite

Why are there ten thousand reasons
That my world is not yours?
Hands, eyes -- yours
My heart shakes in my chest
And birth
Death
Come -- to us
Into any fastness
Desert, mountain, sea,
Galaxy
We take ourselves
As your touch, in freshness,
Touches mine

Lost time take me away
To, as well as from
Love give me
Though I am not here
Kiss my children
And these little poems

Self-conscious, opalescent
We linger among ourselves
In the valleys
Like heavy, white clouds
After the storm clears
Can we grow roses
In this peacefulness --
Have we any peace
Except the peace we are?

As for appearances
Yes
I want them the way they are
Wicked and lovable
Like the smile of Punch
Beckoning us to embrace life
As we would a puppet

Ink bottle people are eloquent
They walk upon my desk
Bearing ink from the well
But most importantly
They are talking to me

Crossed in the back is
As much as crossed on the
                    heart
For you, little girl
In overalls